50 Comfort in Every Bite Recipes

By: Kelly Johnson

Table of Contents

- Mac and Cheese
- Chicken Fried Rice
- Meatloaf with Mashed Potatoes
- Beef Stroganoff
- Chicken and Dumplings
- Baked Ziti
- Shepherd's Pie
- Creamy Tomato Soup with Grilled Cheese
- Homemade Biscuits and Gravy
- Beef Tacos with all the fixings
- Lasagna
- Chicken Parmesan
- Pulled Pork Sandwiches
- Sloppy Joes
- Buffalo Chicken Wings
- Sweet and Sour Pork
- Clam Chowder

- Roast Chicken with Vegetables
- Fried Chicken and Waffles
- Baked Potatoes with Sour Cream and Chives
- Pot Roast with Carrots and Potatoes
- Chili with Cornbread
- Beef and Cheddar Stuffed Potatoes
- Chicken Cacciatore
- Baked Mac and Cheese Cups
- Swedish Meatballs
- Tuna Casserole
- Roasted Sweet Potatoes with Marshmallows
- Gravy-Smothered Chicken
- Poutine
- Beef Enchiladas
- Chicken Tortilla Soup
- Homemade Sausage Gravy with Biscuits
- Broccoli Cheddar Soup
- Pulled BBQ Chicken Sliders
- Pancakes with Maple Syrup

- Eggplant Parmesan
- Sliders with Bacon and Cheese
- Cornbread Stuffing
- French Toast Casserole
- Stuffed Mushrooms
- Chicken Pot Pie Soup
- Sweet and Savory Chicken Skewers
- Crab Cakes with Tartar Sauce
- Baked Sweet Potatoes with Cinnamon Butter
- Egg Salad Sandwiches
- Beef Wellington
- Classic Reuben Sandwich
- Cheesy Potato Casserole
- Chocolate Pudding with Whipped Cream

Mac and Cheese

Ingredients:

- 1 lb elbow macaroni
- 4 cups shredded sharp cheddar cheese
- 1 cup shredded mozzarella cheese
- 2 cups whole milk
- 1/2 cup heavy cream
- 1/4 cup butter
- 1/4 cup all-purpose flour
- 1 tsp mustard powder
- Salt and pepper, to taste
- 1/2 tsp garlic powder (optional)

Instructions:

1. Cook the macaroni according to package instructions. Drain and set aside.
2. In a large saucepan, melt butter over medium heat. Add flour and whisk for 1-2 minutes to create a roux.
3. Slowly add milk and cream, whisking constantly to avoid lumps. Cook until the sauce thickens.
4. Stir in the cheddar and mozzarella cheese, mustard powder, garlic powder, salt, and pepper. Stir until smooth and creamy.
5. Add the cooked macaroni to the sauce and mix well. Serve hot.

Chicken Fried Rice

Ingredients:

- 2 cups cooked rice (preferably day-old)
- 2 chicken breasts, diced
- 2 tbsp soy sauce
- 2 tbsp vegetable oil
- 1/2 cup frozen peas and carrots
- 2 eggs, beaten
- 1/2 onion, diced
- 2 cloves garlic, minced
- 2 green onions, chopped
- Salt and pepper, to taste

Instructions:

1. Heat 1 tbsp of oil in a large skillet or wok over medium-high heat. Add chicken and cook until browned and cooked through. Remove and set aside.
2. In the same pan, add the remaining oil. Cook onion, garlic, peas, and carrots until softened.
3. Push the veggies to the side and scramble the beaten eggs in the pan until cooked.
4. Add the rice, chicken, soy sauce, green onions, salt, and pepper. Stir everything together until heated through.

5. Serve hot.

Meatloaf with Mashed Potatoes

Ingredients for Meatloaf:

- 1 lb ground beef
- 1 egg
- 1/2 cup breadcrumbs
- 1/2 cup milk
- 1 small onion, finely chopped
- 2 tbsp ketchup
- 1 tbsp Worcestershire sauce
- 1 tsp salt
- 1/2 tsp black pepper

Ingredients for Mashed Potatoes:

- 4 large potatoes, peeled and chopped
- 1/2 cup butter
- 1/2 cup milk
- Salt and pepper, to taste

Instructions for Meatloaf:

1. Preheat the oven to 350°F (175°C).

2. In a bowl, combine ground beef, egg, breadcrumbs, milk, onion, ketchup, Worcestershire sauce, salt, and pepper.

3. Form the mixture into a loaf shape and place in a greased baking dish.

4. Bake for 1 hour, or until cooked through.

Instructions for Mashed Potatoes:

1. Boil the potatoes in salted water for 15-20 minutes until tender.

2. Drain and mash the potatoes with butter and milk. Season with salt and pepper to taste.

3. Serve the meatloaf with mashed potatoes.

Beef Stroganoff

Ingredients:

- 1 lb beef sirloin or tenderloin, sliced thin
- 1 onion, chopped
- 2 cloves garlic, minced
- 1/2 cup beef broth
- 1 tbsp flour
- 1 cup sour cream
- 1 tbsp Worcestershire sauce
- 2 tbsp butter
- Salt and pepper, to taste
- Egg noodles, for serving

Instructions:

1. In a skillet, melt butter over medium-high heat. Add the beef and cook until browned. Remove and set aside.

2. In the same skillet, cook onion and garlic until softened.

3. Add flour and stir for 1 minute. Slowly add beef broth, Worcestershire sauce, and stir until thickened.

4. Reduce heat and add sour cream. Stir to combine.

5. Return the beef to the skillet and cook for 2-3 minutes until heated through. Season with salt and pepper.

6. Serve over cooked egg noodles.

Chicken and Dumplings

Ingredients:

- 2 chicken breasts, cooked and shredded
- 1 onion, chopped
- 2 carrots, chopped
- 2 celery stalks, chopped
- 4 cups chicken broth
- 1 tsp thyme
- 2 cups all-purpose flour
- 2 tsp baking powder
- 1/4 cup butter
- 1/2 cup milk
- Salt and pepper, to taste

Instructions:

1. In a large pot, cook onion, carrots, and celery in a little oil until softened.
2. Add chicken broth, thyme, and bring to a boil.
3. In a separate bowl, mix flour, baking powder, butter, and milk to form a dough.
4. Drop spoonfuls of dough into the boiling soup and cook for 10-12 minutes, until dumplings are cooked through.
5. Stir in the shredded chicken and season with salt and pepper. Serve hot.

Baked Ziti

Ingredients:

- 1 lb ziti pasta
- 3 cups marinara sauce
- 2 cups ricotta cheese
- 2 cups shredded mozzarella cheese
- 1/2 cup grated Parmesan cheese
- 1 tsp dried basil
- 1 tsp dried oregano
- Salt and pepper, to taste

Instructions:

1. Preheat the oven to 375°F (190°C).
2. Cook the ziti pasta according to package directions, then drain.
3. In a large bowl, combine pasta, marinara sauce, ricotta cheese, mozzarella, Parmesan, basil, oregano, salt, and pepper.
4. Transfer to a baking dish and bake for 25-30 minutes, until the cheese is melted and bubbly.
5. Serve hot.

Shepherd's Pie

Ingredients:

- 1 lb ground beef or lamb
- 1 onion, chopped
- 2 carrots, chopped
- 2 cups frozen peas
- 2 cups mashed potatoes (prepared)
- 1/4 cup beef broth
- 1 tbsp Worcestershire sauce
- Salt and pepper, to taste

Instructions:

1. In a skillet, cook ground beef or lamb with onion and carrots until browned and softened.
2. Add peas, beef broth, Worcestershire sauce, salt, and pepper. Simmer for 5 minutes.
3. Transfer the meat mixture into a baking dish and spread the mashed potatoes on top.
4. Bake at 375°F (190°C) for 20-25 minutes, until the top is golden.
5. Serve hot.

Creamy Tomato Soup with Grilled Cheese

Ingredients for Tomato Soup:

- 1 can (28 oz) crushed tomatoes
- 1 onion, chopped
- 2 cloves garlic, minced
- 1 cup chicken broth
- 1/2 cup heavy cream
- 1 tbsp olive oil
- Salt and pepper, to taste
- Fresh basil (optional)

Ingredients for Grilled Cheese:

- 8 slices bread
- 4 slices cheddar cheese
- 4 tbsp butter

Instructions for Soup:

1. In a pot, cook onion and garlic in olive oil until softened.
2. Add crushed tomatoes and chicken broth, bring to a simmer for 20 minutes.
3. Stir in heavy cream and season with salt and pepper. Blend with an immersion blender for smoothness.

4. Serve with fresh basil, if desired.

Instructions for Grilled Cheese:

1. Butter the outside of each slice of bread and place cheese in the middle.

2. Grill the sandwiches in a pan until golden brown on both sides.

3. Serve with tomato soup.

Homemade Biscuits and Gravy

Ingredients for Biscuits:

- 2 cups all-purpose flour
- 1 tbsp baking powder
- 1/2 tsp salt
- 1/2 cup cold butter
- 3/4 cup milk

Ingredients for Gravy:

- 1 lb sausage (breakfast or Italian)
- 1/4 cup all-purpose flour
- 2 cups milk
- Salt and pepper, to taste

Instructions for Biscuits:

1. Preheat the oven to 450°F (230°C).
2. In a bowl, mix flour, baking powder, and salt. Cut in cold butter until the mixture resembles crumbs.
3. Stir in milk until the dough forms. Roll out and cut into biscuits.
4. Bake for 12-15 minutes until golden brown.

Instructions for Gravy:

1. Brown sausage in a pan until fully cooked. Remove excess grease.

2. Stir in flour and cook for 1-2 minutes.

3. Gradually add milk, whisking to avoid lumps. Simmer until thickened.

4. Season with salt and pepper, then serve over biscuits.

Beef Tacos with All the Fixings

Ingredients:

- 1 lb ground beef
- 1 packet taco seasoning
- 1/2 cup water
- 8 taco shells
- Lettuce, chopped
- Tomatoes, diced
- Shredded cheddar cheese
- Sour cream
- Salsa

Instructions:

1. Cook ground beef in a pan, then drain excess grease.
2. Add taco seasoning and water. Simmer for 5 minutes.
3. Warm taco shells and fill with beef mixture.
4. Top with lettuce, tomatoes, cheese, sour cream, and salsa.

Lasagna

Ingredients:

- 1 lb ground beef or sausage
- 1 onion, chopped
- 2 cloves garlic, minced
- 3 cups marinara sauce
- 12 lasagna noodles, cooked
- 3 cups ricotta cheese
- 2 cups shredded mozzarella cheese
- 1/4 cup grated Parmesan cheese
- 1 egg
- 1 tbsp dried basil
- Salt and pepper, to taste

Instructions:

1. Preheat the oven to 375°F (190°C).
2. Brown ground beef or sausage with onion and garlic. Add marinara sauce and simmer.
3. Mix ricotta cheese, mozzarella, Parmesan, egg, basil, salt, and pepper.
4. Layer noodles, sauce, and cheese mixture in a baking dish.
5. Bake for 45 minutes, then let rest for 10 minutes before serving.

Chicken Parmesan

Ingredients:

- 4 boneless, skinless chicken breasts
- 1 cup all-purpose flour
- 2 eggs, beaten
- 1 1/2 cups breadcrumbs
- 1 cup grated Parmesan cheese
- 2 cups marinara sauce
- 2 cups shredded mozzarella cheese
- 1/4 cup olive oil
- Salt and pepper, to taste
- Fresh basil (optional)

Instructions:

1. Preheat the oven to 375°F (190°C).

2. Season the chicken breasts with salt and pepper. Dredge each chicken breast in flour, then dip in beaten eggs, and coat with breadcrumbs mixed with Parmesan cheese.

3. Heat olive oil in a large skillet over medium heat. Brown the chicken breasts on both sides until golden (about 3-4 minutes per side).

4. Transfer the chicken breasts to a baking dish. Top each with marinara sauce and mozzarella cheese.

5. Bake for 20-25 minutes, or until the chicken is cooked through and the cheese is melted and bubbly.

6. Serve with fresh basil and pasta, if desired.

Pulled Pork Sandwiches

Ingredients:

- 3-4 lb pork shoulder
- 1 cup barbecue sauce
- 1 onion, chopped
- 2 cloves garlic, minced
- 1 tsp paprika
- 1 tsp chili powder
- 1/2 tsp cumin
- Salt and pepper, to taste
- 8 hamburger buns

Instructions:

1. Rub the pork shoulder with paprika, chili powder, cumin, salt, and pepper.
2. Place the pork in a slow cooker with onion, garlic, and 1/2 cup barbecue sauce. Cook on low for 6-8 hours until tender.
3. Shred the pork with two forks. Add the remaining barbecue sauce and stir to combine.
4. Serve on hamburger buns with additional barbecue sauce, pickles, and coleslaw.

Sloppy Joes

Ingredients:

- 1 lb ground beef
- 1 onion, chopped
- 1 bell pepper, chopped
- 1 can (8 oz) tomato sauce
- 1/4 cup ketchup
- 2 tbsp Worcestershire sauce
- 1 tbsp brown sugar
- 1 tbsp mustard
- Salt and pepper, to taste
- 4 hamburger buns

Instructions:

1. In a skillet, cook ground beef over medium heat until browned. Drain excess fat.
2. Add onion and bell pepper to the skillet and cook until softened.
3. Stir in tomato sauce, ketchup, Worcestershire sauce, brown sugar, mustard, salt, and pepper. Simmer for 10 minutes, stirring occasionally.
4. Serve the sloppy joe mixture on hamburger buns.

Buffalo Chicken Wings

Ingredients:

- 12 chicken wings
- 1/2 cup hot sauce
- 1/4 cup butter, melted
- 1 tbsp white vinegar
- 1/4 tsp garlic powder
- Salt and pepper, to taste
- Ranch or blue cheese dressing, for serving

Instructions:

1. Preheat the oven to 400°F (200°C). Place the chicken wings on a baking sheet and season with salt and pepper.
2. Bake for 25-30 minutes, turning halfway, until crispy and cooked through.
3. In a bowl, mix hot sauce, melted butter, vinegar, and garlic powder.
4. Toss the cooked wings in the buffalo sauce and serve with ranch or blue cheese dressing.

Sweet and Sour Pork

Ingredients:

- 1 lb pork tenderloin, cut into 1-inch cubes
- 1/2 cup cornstarch
- 1/2 cup vegetable oil
- 1/2 onion, chopped
- 1 bell pepper, chopped
- 1/2 cup pineapple chunks
- 1/4 cup vinegar
- 1/4 cup sugar
- 1/4 cup ketchup
- 2 tbsp soy sauce
- Salt and pepper, to taste

Instructions:

1. Toss the pork cubes in cornstarch until evenly coated.
2. Heat vegetable oil in a large skillet over medium-high heat. Cook the pork until browned and cooked through. Remove and set aside.
3. In the same skillet, sauté onion and bell pepper until softened.
4. In a bowl, mix vinegar, sugar, ketchup, soy sauce, salt, and pepper. Pour the mixture into the skillet and bring to a simmer.

5. Add pineapple chunks and the cooked pork. Stir to coat and cook for another 5 minutes.

6. Serve with rice.

Clam Chowder

Ingredients:

- 4 cups potatoes, peeled and diced
- 1 onion, chopped
- 2 celery stalks, chopped
- 2 cloves garlic, minced
- 4 cups clam broth
- 1 can (6.5 oz) clams, drained
- 2 cups heavy cream
- 1/4 cup butter
- Salt and pepper, to taste
- Fresh parsley (optional)

Instructions:

1. In a large pot, melt butter over medium heat. Cook onion, celery, and garlic until softened.
2. Add the diced potatoes and clam broth. Simmer until potatoes are tender (about 15-20 minutes).
3. Add the clams and heavy cream, then cook for an additional 5 minutes. Season with salt and pepper.
4. Serve with fresh parsley, if desired.

Roast Chicken with Vegetables

Ingredients:

- 1 whole chicken (about 4-5 lbs)
- 2 tbsp olive oil
- 1 tbsp rosemary
- 1 tbsp thyme
- 1 lemon, halved
- 1 onion, quartered
- 4 carrots, peeled and cut into chunks
- 4 potatoes, peeled and cut into chunks
- Salt and pepper, to taste

Instructions:

1. Preheat the oven to 425°F (220°C).
2. Rub the chicken with olive oil, rosemary, thyme, salt, and pepper. Place the lemon halves and onion quarters inside the chicken cavity.
3. Arrange the carrots and potatoes around the chicken in a roasting pan.
4. Roast for 1 hour and 20 minutes, or until the chicken reaches an internal temperature of 165°F (75°C) and the vegetables are tender.
5. Let the chicken rest for 10 minutes before carving. Serve with roasted vegetables.

Fried Chicken and Waffles

Ingredients for Fried Chicken:

- 4 chicken pieces (drumsticks, thighs, or breasts)
- 1 cup buttermilk
- 1 cup all-purpose flour
- 1 tbsp paprika
- 1 tsp garlic powder
- Salt and pepper, to taste
- Vegetable oil, for frying

Ingredients for Waffles:

- 2 cups all-purpose flour
- 2 tbsp sugar
- 2 tsp baking powder
- 1/2 tsp salt
- 2 eggs
- 1 1/2 cups milk
- 1/4 cup melted butter
- 1 tsp vanilla extract

Instructions for Fried Chicken:

1. Marinate chicken pieces in buttermilk for at least 2 hours or overnight.

2. In a bowl, mix flour, paprika, garlic powder, salt, and pepper.

3. Heat oil in a skillet to 350°F (175°C). Dredge each piece of chicken in the flour mixture and fry until golden and cooked through, about 12-15 minutes.

4. Remove and drain on paper towels.

Instructions for Waffles:

1. Preheat a waffle iron. In a bowl, mix flour, sugar, baking powder, and salt.

2. Whisk eggs, milk, melted butter, and vanilla in another bowl. Combine with dry ingredients until smooth.

3. Pour the batter into the waffle iron and cook according to the manufacturer's instructions.

4. Serve the fried chicken on top of waffles with syrup.

Baked Potatoes with Sour Cream and Chives

Ingredients:

- 4 large russet potatoes
- Olive oil
- Salt
- 1/2 cup sour cream
- 2 tbsp chives, chopped
- Butter (optional)

Instructions:

1. Preheat the oven to 400°F (200°C).
2. Rub the potatoes with olive oil and sprinkle with salt. Pierce the potatoes several times with a fork.
3. Bake for 45-60 minutes, or until the potatoes are soft.
4. Slice open and top with sour cream, chives, and butter.

Pot Roast with Carrots and Potatoes

Ingredients:

- 3-4 lb chuck roast
- 4 carrots, peeled and cut into chunks
- 4 potatoes, peeled and cut into chunks
- 1 onion, chopped
- 2 cloves garlic, minced
- 4 cups beef broth
- 1 tbsp Worcestershire sauce
- 1 tbsp rosemary
- Salt and pepper, to taste

Instructions:

1. Preheat the oven to 325°F (160°C).
2. Season the roast with salt and pepper. Brown the roast in a large oven-safe pot over medium-high heat.
3. Remove the roast and sauté onion and garlic in the same pot. Add beef broth, Worcestershire sauce, and rosemary.
4. Return the roast to the pot. Add carrots and potatoes around the roast.
5. Cover and bake for 3-4 hours, until the roast is tender and the vegetables are cooked.
6. Serve hot.

Chili with Cornbread

Ingredients for Chili:

- 1 lb ground beef
- 1 onion, chopped
- 2 cloves garlic, minced
- 1 can (15 oz) kidney beans, drained and rinsed
- 1 can (15 oz) diced tomatoes
- 1 can (6 oz) tomato paste
- 2 tbsp chili powder
- 1 tsp cumin
- 1/2 tsp paprika
- Salt and pepper, to taste
- 1 cup beef broth

Ingredients for Cornbread:

- 1 cup all-purpose flour
- 1 cup cornmeal
- 1/4 cup sugar
- 1 tbsp baking powder
- 1/2 tsp salt

- 1 cup milk

- 2 eggs

- 1/4 cup butter, melted

Instructions for Chili:

1. In a large pot, cook ground beef over medium heat until browned. Remove any excess fat.

2. Add onion and garlic to the pot, cooking until softened.

3. Stir in kidney beans, diced tomatoes, tomato paste, chili powder, cumin, paprika, salt, and pepper.

4. Pour in beef broth and bring the mixture to a simmer. Cook for 30 minutes, stirring occasionally.

5. Adjust seasoning to taste.

Instructions for Cornbread:

1. Preheat the oven to 375°F (190°C). Grease a baking dish or an 8x8-inch pan.

2. In a large bowl, combine flour, cornmeal, sugar, baking powder, and salt.

3. In another bowl, whisk together milk, eggs, and melted butter. Pour the wet ingredients into the dry ingredients and mix until just combined.

4. Pour the batter into the prepared pan and bake for 25-30 minutes, or until golden brown and a toothpick inserted comes out clean.

5. Serve the chili with a side of cornbread.

Beef and Cheddar Stuffed Potatoes

Ingredients:

- 4 large russet potatoes
- 1 lb ground beef
- 1 onion, chopped
- 1 cup shredded cheddar cheese
- 1/4 cup sour cream
- 2 tbsp butter
- Salt and pepper, to taste
- Green onions, chopped (for garnish)

Instructions:

1. Preheat the oven to 400°F (200°C). Pierce the potatoes with a fork and bake for 45-60 minutes, until tender.
2. While the potatoes bake, cook ground beef in a skillet over medium heat until browned. Add chopped onion and cook until softened.
3. Cut the baked potatoes in half and scoop out the flesh into a bowl, leaving a small border around the edges.
4. Mash the potato flesh with butter, sour cream, salt, and pepper. Stir in the cooked beef mixture and half of the cheddar cheese.
5. Spoon the mixture back into the potato skins and top with the remaining cheddar cheese.

6. Return the stuffed potatoes to the oven for 10-15 minutes, until the cheese is melted and bubbly.

7. Garnish with chopped green onions and serve.

Chicken Cacciatore

Ingredients:

- 4 bone-in, skinless chicken thighs
- 1 onion, chopped
- 2 cloves garlic, minced
- 1 bell pepper, chopped
- 1 can (14.5 oz) diced tomatoes
- 1/2 cup dry white wine
- 1/2 cup chicken broth
- 1 tsp dried oregano
- 1 tsp dried basil
- Salt and pepper, to taste
- Fresh parsley, chopped (for garnish)

Instructions:

1. Heat olive oil in a large skillet over medium-high heat. Season chicken thighs with salt and pepper, then brown them on both sides for about 5-7 minutes.

2. Remove the chicken from the skillet and set aside. In the same skillet, sauté onion, garlic, and bell pepper until softened.

3. Add diced tomatoes, white wine, chicken broth, oregano, basil, salt, and pepper. Stir to combine.

4. Return the chicken to the skillet and cover. Simmer for 30-40 minutes, or until the chicken is fully cooked and tender.

5. Garnish with chopped parsley and serve over pasta or rice.

Baked Mac and Cheese Cups

Ingredients:

- 2 cups elbow macaroni, cooked
- 1 1/2 cups shredded cheddar cheese
- 1/2 cup grated Parmesan cheese
- 1 cup milk
- 1 egg
- 2 tbsp butter, melted
- 1 tbsp flour
- 1 tsp mustard powder
- Salt and pepper, to taste
- Bread crumbs (for topping)

Instructions:

1. Preheat the oven to 375°F (190°C) and grease a muffin tin.
2. In a saucepan, melt butter over medium heat. Stir in flour and mustard powder to make a roux. Gradually add milk, whisking until smooth. Cook for 2-3 minutes until thickened.
3. Remove from heat and stir in the cheddar cheese, Parmesan cheese, salt, and pepper.
4. In a bowl, whisk the egg, then add it to the sauce mixture. Stir in the cooked macaroni.

5. Spoon the mac and cheese mixture into the muffin tin, filling each cup about 3/4 full. Top with bread crumbs.

6. Bake for 15-20 minutes, until golden and bubbly. Let cool slightly before serving.

Swedish Meatballs

Ingredients for Meatballs:

- 1 lb ground beef
- 1/2 lb ground pork
- 1/4 cup bread crumbs
- 1/4 cup milk
- 1 egg
- 1/2 tsp onion powder
- 1/2 tsp garlic powder
- Salt and pepper, to taste

Ingredients for Gravy:

- 2 tbsp butter
- 2 tbsp all-purpose flour
- 2 cups beef broth
- 1/4 cup heavy cream
- 1 tbsp soy sauce
- Salt and pepper, to taste

Instructions for Meatballs:

1. Preheat the oven to 375°F (190°C). Line a baking sheet with parchment paper.

2. In a large bowl, combine ground beef, ground pork, bread crumbs, milk, egg, onion powder, garlic powder, salt, and pepper. Mix until well combined.

3. Roll the mixture into small meatballs (about 1 inch in diameter) and place them on the prepared baking sheet.

4. Bake for 15-20 minutes, or until the meatballs are cooked through.

Instructions for Gravy:

1. In a saucepan, melt butter over medium heat. Stir in flour and cook for 1-2 minutes to make a roux.

2. Gradually add beef broth, whisking constantly. Cook for 3-4 minutes until the sauce thickens.

3. Stir in heavy cream, soy sauce, salt, and pepper. Simmer for another 2-3 minutes.

4. Pour the gravy over the meatballs and serve with mashed potatoes or egg noodles.

Tuna Casserole

Ingredients:

- 2 cans (5 oz each) tuna, drained
- 1 cup cooked egg noodles
- 1 can (10.5 oz) cream of mushroom soup
- 1/2 cup milk
- 1 cup frozen peas
- 1/2 cup shredded cheddar cheese
- 1/2 cup bread crumbs
- Salt and pepper, to taste

Instructions:

1. Preheat the oven to 350°F (175°C). Grease a 9x9-inch baking dish.
2. In a bowl, combine tuna, cooked egg noodles, cream of mushroom soup, milk, peas, and half of the cheddar cheese. Season with salt and pepper.
3. Pour the mixture into the prepared baking dish and top with the remaining cheddar cheese and bread crumbs.
4. Bake for 25-30 minutes, until the casserole is hot and bubbly.

Roasted Sweet Potatoes with Marshmallows

Ingredients:

- 4 large sweet potatoes, peeled and cubed
- 2 tbsp olive oil
- 1/4 tsp cinnamon
- 1/4 tsp nutmeg
- Salt and pepper, to taste
- 1 cup mini marshmallows

Instructions:

1. Preheat the oven to 400°F (200°C).
2. Toss the sweet potatoes with olive oil, cinnamon, nutmeg, salt, and pepper. Spread them in a single layer on a baking sheet.
3. Roast for 25-30 minutes, until tender.
4. Remove from the oven, top with marshmallows, and return to the oven for an additional 5 minutes, until the marshmallows are golden brown.

Gravy-Smothered Chicken

Ingredients:

- 4 boneless, skinless chicken breasts
- 1/2 cup flour
- 1 tbsp paprika
- Salt and pepper, to taste
- 2 tbsp olive oil
- 2 cups chicken broth
- 1/2 cup heavy cream
- 1/4 tsp thyme

Instructions:

1. Season chicken breasts with salt, pepper, and paprika. Dredge them in flour, shaking off any excess.

2. Heat olive oil in a skillet over medium-high heat. Cook the chicken for 6-7 minutes per side, until golden brown and cooked through. Remove the chicken and set aside.

3. In the same skillet, add chicken broth, heavy cream, and thyme. Stir to combine, scraping up any browned bits from the bottom of the pan.

4. Bring the sauce to a simmer and cook for 5 minutes until thickened.

5. Pour the gravy over the chicken and serve.

Poutine

Ingredients:

- 4 cups French fries (store-bought or homemade)
- 2 cups cheese curds
- 1 1/2 cups brown gravy (homemade or store-bought)

Instructions:

1. Cook the French fries according to the package instructions or make homemade fries.
2. While the fries are cooking, heat the brown gravy in a saucepan.
3. Once the fries are ready, top them with cheese curds and pour hot gravy over the top.
4. Serve immediately.

Beef Enchiladas

Ingredients:

- 1 lb ground beef
- 1 onion, chopped
- 1 can (10 oz) enchilada sauce
- 1 cup shredded cheddar cheese
- 8 flour tortillas
- 1/2 tsp cumin
- 1/2 tsp chili powder
- Salt and pepper, to taste

Instructions:

1. Preheat the oven to 350°F (175°C). Grease a baking dish.
2. In a skillet, cook ground beef and onion until browned. Stir in cumin, chili powder, salt, and pepper.
3. Add half of the enchilada sauce and stir to combine.
4. Fill each tortilla with the beef mixture and roll it up. Place the rolled tortillas in the prepared baking dish.
5. Pour the remaining enchilada sauce over the top and sprinkle with shredded cheese.
6. Bake for 20-25 minutes, until the cheese is melted and bubbly.

Chicken Tortilla Soup

Ingredients:

- 1 lb chicken breast or thighs, cooked and shredded
- 1 onion, chopped
- 2 cloves garlic, minced
- 1 can (15 oz) diced tomatoes
- 1 can (4 oz) green chilies
- 1 can (15 oz) black beans, drained and rinsed
- 4 cups chicken broth
- 1 tsp cumin
- 1 tsp chili powder
- Salt and pepper, to taste
- 1 cup frozen corn
- 1 tbsp lime juice
- Tortilla strips or chips, for garnish
- Shredded cheese, sour cream, and avocado for toppings

Instructions:

1. In a large pot, sauté the onion and garlic in a little oil until softened.
2. Add diced tomatoes, green chilies, black beans, chicken broth, cumin, chili powder, salt, and pepper. Bring to a simmer and cook for 15 minutes.

3. Stir in the shredded chicken and frozen corn, and cook for another 5-7 minutes until heated through.

4. Add lime juice and adjust seasoning to taste.

5. Serve with tortilla strips or chips and top with shredded cheese, sour cream, and avocado.

Homemade Sausage Gravy with Biscuits

Ingredients for Sausage Gravy:

- 1 lb breakfast sausage
- 2 tbsp flour
- 2 cups milk
- Salt and pepper, to taste
- 1/4 tsp crushed red pepper flakes (optional)

Ingredients for Biscuits:

- 2 cups all-purpose flour
- 1 tbsp baking powder
- 1/2 tsp salt
- 1/2 cup cold butter, cubed
- 3/4 cup milk

Instructions for Sausage Gravy:

1. In a skillet, crumble and cook sausage over medium heat until browned and cooked through.
2. Sprinkle flour over the sausage and stir to coat. Cook for 1-2 minutes.
3. Gradually add milk, stirring constantly, and cook for 5-7 minutes until the gravy thickens. Season with salt, pepper, and red pepper flakes, if desired.
4. Keep warm on low heat while you prepare the biscuits.

Instructions for Biscuits:

1. Preheat the oven to 450°F (230°C). Grease a baking sheet.

2. In a large bowl, combine flour, baking powder, and salt. Cut in the butter until the mixture resembles coarse crumbs.

3. Stir in milk until just combined (do not overmix).

4. Turn the dough onto a floured surface, knead gently a few times, then roll out to 1-inch thickness.

5. Cut out biscuits with a round cutter and place them on the baking sheet.

6. Bake for 10-12 minutes, or until golden brown.

7. Serve the biscuits with sausage gravy.

Broccoli Cheddar Soup

Ingredients:

- 1 tbsp olive oil
- 1 onion, chopped
- 2 cloves garlic, minced
- 4 cups broccoli florets
- 3 cups chicken or vegetable broth
- 2 cups milk
- 2 cups shredded cheddar cheese
- 2 tbsp butter
- 1/4 cup flour
- Salt and pepper, to taste

Instructions:

1. In a large pot, heat olive oil and sauté onion and garlic until softened.
2. Add broccoli and broth, and bring to a boil. Reduce heat and simmer for 15-20 minutes until broccoli is tender.
3. In a separate saucepan, melt butter and whisk in flour to make a roux. Cook for 1-2 minutes.
4. Gradually add milk to the roux, stirring constantly, until the mixture thickens (about 3-4 minutes).

5. Pour the milk mixture into the soup, stir to combine, and cook for another 5 minutes.

6. Add shredded cheddar cheese and stir until melted. Season with salt and pepper to taste.

7. Serve warm with extra cheese on top.

Pulled BBQ Chicken Sliders

Ingredients:

- 1 lb chicken breast, cooked and shredded
- 1 cup BBQ sauce
- 12 slider buns
- 1/2 cup coleslaw (optional)

Instructions:

1. In a saucepan, heat the shredded chicken with BBQ sauce over medium heat until warmed through.
2. Split the slider buns and toast lightly if desired.
3. Spoon the BBQ chicken mixture onto each bun.
4. Top with coleslaw if using and serve.

Pancakes with Maple Syrup

Ingredients:

- 1 cup all-purpose flour
- 2 tbsp sugar
- 1 tbsp baking powder
- 1/4 tsp salt
- 1 cup milk
- 1 egg
- 2 tbsp melted butter
- 1 tsp vanilla extract
- Maple syrup, for serving

Instructions:

1. In a large bowl, whisk together flour, sugar, baking powder, and salt.
2. In another bowl, beat together milk, egg, melted butter, and vanilla extract.
3. Pour the wet ingredients into the dry ingredients and stir until just combined (lumps are okay).
4. Heat a griddle or skillet over medium heat and lightly grease.
5. Pour about 1/4 cup of batter for each pancake onto the griddle. Cook until bubbles form on the surface, then flip and cook the other side until golden brown.
6. Serve with maple syrup.

Eggplant Parmesan

Ingredients:

- 2 medium eggplants, sliced into 1/2-inch thick rounds
- Salt, for sweating the eggplant
- 2 cups marinara sauce
- 1 1/2 cups shredded mozzarella cheese
- 1/2 cup grated Parmesan cheese
- 1 cup breadcrumbs
- 1/2 cup all-purpose flour
- 2 eggs, beaten
- Olive oil, for frying

Instructions:

1. Sprinkle the eggplant slices with salt and let them sit for 30 minutes to draw out moisture. Pat them dry with paper towels.
2. Preheat oven to 375°F (190°C).
3. Dredge the eggplant slices in flour, then dip into beaten eggs, and coat with breadcrumbs.
4. Heat olive oil in a skillet over medium heat. Fry the eggplant slices until golden brown, about 2-3 minutes per side.
5. In a baking dish, spread a thin layer of marinara sauce. Layer the fried eggplant slices, sauce, mozzarella, and Parmesan cheese. Repeat until all ingredients are used.

6. Top with cheese and bake for 20-25 minutes until bubbly and golden. Serve with pasta or garlic bread.

Sliders with Bacon and Cheese

Ingredients:

- 1 lb ground beef
- 1/4 cup breadcrumbs
- 1 egg
- Salt and pepper, to taste
- 6 slider buns
- 6 slices cheddar cheese
- 6 slices cooked bacon

Instructions:

1. Preheat the grill or a skillet over medium-high heat.
2. In a bowl, mix ground beef, breadcrumbs, egg, salt, and pepper. Form into 6 small patties.
3. Cook the patties for 4-5 minutes per side until cooked through.
4. During the last minute of cooking, place a slice of cheese on each patty and let it melt.
5. Assemble the sliders by placing a patty on each bun and topping with a slice of bacon.
6. Serve immediately.

Cornbread Stuffing

Ingredients:

- 1 batch cornbread, crumbled
- 1 onion, chopped
- 2 celery stalks, chopped
- 2 cloves garlic, minced
- 2 cups chicken broth
- 1/4 cup butter
- 1 tsp dried sage
- 1 tsp thyme
- Salt and pepper, to taste

Instructions:

1. Preheat the oven to 350°F (175°C).
2. In a large skillet, melt butter over medium heat. Sauté onion, celery, and garlic until softened.
3. In a large bowl, combine the crumbled cornbread with the sautéed vegetables, sage, thyme, salt, and pepper.
4. Gradually add chicken broth until the mixture is moist but not soggy.
5. Transfer to a greased baking dish and bake for 25-30 minutes, until golden and crispy on top.

French Toast Casserole

Ingredients:

- 8 slices bread (day-old works best)
- 4 eggs
- 2 cups milk
- 1/4 cup sugar
- 1 tsp vanilla extract
- 1/2 tsp cinnamon
- 1/4 tsp nutmeg
- Maple syrup, for serving

Instructions:

1. Preheat the oven to 350°F (175°C) and grease a 9x13-inch baking dish.
2. Cut the bread into cubes and place them in the prepared baking dish.
3. In a bowl, whisk together eggs, milk, sugar, vanilla, cinnamon, and nutmeg. Pour over the bread cubes.
4. Press the bread down slightly to ensure it absorbs the liquid. Cover and refrigerate for at least 30 minutes or overnight.
5. Bake for 40-45 minutes, until golden brown. Serve with maple syrup.

Stuffed Mushrooms

Ingredients:

- 16 large button mushrooms, stems removed
- 1/2 lb sausage, crumbled
- 1/4 cup breadcrumbs
- 1/4 cup grated Parmesan cheese
- 1/4 cup cream cheese, softened
- 2 tbsp fresh parsley, chopped

Instructions:

1. Preheat the oven to 375°F (190°C). Grease a baking sheet.
2. In a skillet, cook the sausage until browned. Remove from heat and mix in breadcrumbs, Parmesan, cream cheese, and parsley.
3. Stuff the mushroom caps with the sausage mixture and place on the baking sheet.
4. Bake for 15-20 minutes until the mushrooms are tender and the filling is golden.

Chicken Pot Pie Soup

Ingredients:

- 1 lb cooked chicken, shredded
- 1 onion, chopped
- 2 carrots, chopped
- 2 celery stalks, chopped
- 2 cups chicken broth
- 1 cup heavy cream
- 2 cups frozen peas
- 1 tsp thyme
- 2 tbsp flour
- Salt and pepper, to taste

Instructions:

1. In a large pot, sauté onion, carrots, and celery until softened.
2. Sprinkle flour over the vegetables and cook for 1-2 minutes.
3. Gradually add chicken broth and heavy cream, stirring constantly until the mixture thickens.
4. Stir in the chicken, peas, thyme, salt, and pepper. Simmer for 10-15 minutes.
5. Serve with crusty bread.

Sweet and Savory Chicken Skewers

Ingredients:

- 1 lb chicken breast, cut into cubes
- 1/4 cup soy sauce
- 2 tbsp honey
- 2 tbsp olive oil
- 1 tsp garlic powder
- 1 tsp ginger powder
- 1/2 tsp black pepper
- Wooden skewers, soaked in water

Instructions:

1. In a bowl, whisk together soy sauce, honey, olive oil, garlic powder, ginger powder, and black pepper.
2. Thread the chicken cubes onto the soaked skewers and brush with the marinade.
3. Grill the skewers over medium-high heat for 5-7 minutes per side, until fully cooked.
4. Serve with rice or vegetables.

Crab Cakes with Tartar Sauce

Ingredients for Crab Cakes:

- 1 lb lump crab meat, drained and picked through
- 1/2 cup breadcrumbs
- 1/4 cup mayonnaise
- 1 egg
- 1 tbsp Dijon mustard
- 1 tbsp Worcestershire sauce
- 1 tsp Old Bay seasoning
- 2 tbsp fresh parsley, chopped
- Salt and pepper, to taste
- 2 tbsp olive oil (for frying)

Ingredients for Tartar Sauce:

- 1/2 cup mayonnaise
- 2 tbsp dill relish
- 1 tbsp lemon juice
- 1 tsp Dijon mustard
- Salt and pepper, to taste

Instructions for Crab Cakes:

1. In a bowl, combine crab meat, breadcrumbs, mayonnaise, egg, mustard, Worcestershire sauce, Old Bay seasoning, parsley, salt, and pepper.

2. Gently mix until well combined, being careful not to break up the crab meat too much.

3. Form the mixture into 8 small patties.

4. Heat olive oil in a skillet over medium heat. Fry the crab cakes for about 3-4 minutes per side, until golden brown and crispy.

5. For the tartar sauce, mix together mayonnaise, dill relish, lemon juice, Dijon mustard, salt, and pepper.

6. Serve the crab cakes with tartar sauce on the side.

Baked Sweet Potatoes with Cinnamon Butter

Ingredients:

- 4 medium sweet potatoes
- 1/4 cup butter, softened
- 1 tsp cinnamon
- 1 tbsp brown sugar
- 1/4 tsp salt

Instructions:

1. Preheat the oven to 400°F (200°C).
2. Pierce the sweet potatoes with a fork several times, then place them on a baking sheet.
3. Bake for 45-60 minutes, or until the sweet potatoes are tender when pierced with a fork.
4. While the potatoes are baking, mix softened butter, cinnamon, brown sugar, and salt in a bowl.
5. Once the sweet potatoes are done, slice them open and top with the cinnamon butter.
6. Serve warm.

Egg Salad Sandwiches

Ingredients:

- 6 large eggs, boiled and chopped
- 1/4 cup mayonnaise
- 1 tsp Dijon mustard
- 1 tbsp fresh dill, chopped (optional)
- Salt and pepper, to taste
- 8 slices bread (your choice)
- Lettuce leaves (optional)

Instructions:

1. Boil the eggs and peel them once cooled. Chop them into small pieces.
2. In a bowl, combine the chopped eggs, mayonnaise, mustard, dill (if using), salt, and pepper. Mix well.
3. Spread the egg salad onto slices of bread and add a lettuce leaf, if desired.
4. Serve immediately or refrigerate until ready to serve.

Beef Wellington

Ingredients:

- 1 lb beef tenderloin (center cut)
- Salt and pepper, to taste
- 2 tbsp olive oil
- 1/4 cup Dijon mustard
- 8 oz cremini or white mushrooms, finely chopped
- 2 tbsp butter
- 2 tbsp fresh thyme, chopped
- 1/4 cup dry white wine (optional)
- 1 package puff pastry (2 sheets)
- 1 egg, beaten (for egg wash)

Instructions:

1. Preheat the oven to 400°F (200°C).

2. Season the beef tenderloin with salt and pepper. Heat olive oil in a large skillet over medium-high heat, and sear the beef on all sides until browned (about 2-3 minutes per side).

3. Remove the beef from the skillet and brush with Dijon mustard. Let it cool.

4. In the same skillet, melt butter over medium heat and cook the mushrooms and thyme until the mushrooms release their moisture and become soft, about 10 minutes. If using, add white wine and cook until the mixture is dry.

5. Roll out the puff pastry on a lightly floured surface. Place the mushroom mixture in the center of the pastry and top with the beef. Fold the pastry over the beef and seal the edges.

6. Brush the pastry with the beaten egg wash.

7. Bake for 25-30 minutes, until the pastry is golden brown and the beef reaches your desired level of doneness (use a meat thermometer for accuracy).

8. Let the Beef Wellington rest for 10 minutes before slicing and serving.

Classic Reuben Sandwich

Ingredients:

- 8 slices rye bread
- 1/2 lb corned beef, thinly sliced
- 4 slices Swiss cheese
- 1/4 cup sauerkraut, drained
- 1/4 cup thousand island dressing or Russian dressing
- Butter, for grilling

Instructions:

1. Heat a griddle or skillet over medium heat.
2. Spread dressing on one side of each slice of rye bread.
3. On four slices of bread, layer corned beef, Swiss cheese, and sauerkraut. Top with the remaining slices of bread, dressing side down.
4. Butter the outside of the sandwiches and grill them on the griddle until golden brown and the cheese is melted, about 3-4 minutes per side.
5. Serve hot and enjoy!

Cheesy Potato Casserole

Ingredients:

- 4 cups frozen hash browns, thawed
- 1 can (10.5 oz) cream of mushroom soup
- 1/2 cup sour cream
- 1/4 cup butter, melted
- 2 cups shredded cheddar cheese
- 1/4 cup grated Parmesan cheese
- Salt and pepper, to taste
- 1/2 cup cornflakes (optional)

Instructions:

1. Preheat the oven to 350°F (175°C). Grease a 9x13-inch baking dish.
2. In a large bowl, mix together hash browns, cream of mushroom soup, sour cream, melted butter, shredded cheddar, Parmesan cheese, salt, and pepper.
3. Spread the mixture evenly in the prepared baking dish.
4. If using cornflakes, sprinkle them over the top for extra crunch.
5. Bake for 45-50 minutes, until the casserole is hot and bubbly, and the top is golden brown.
6. Serve warm.

Chocolate Pudding with Whipped Cream

Ingredients for Chocolate Pudding:

- 1/2 cup granulated sugar
- 1/3 cup unsweetened cocoa powder
- 1/4 cup cornstarch
- 1/8 tsp salt
- 2 3/4 cups milk
- 1 tsp vanilla extract
- 2 tbsp butter

Ingredients for Whipped Cream:

- 1 cup heavy cream
- 2 tbsp powdered sugar
- 1/2 tsp vanilla extract

Instructions for Chocolate Pudding:

1. In a saucepan, whisk together sugar, cocoa powder, cornstarch, and salt.
2. Gradually add milk while whisking to combine. Cook over medium heat, whisking constantly, until the pudding thickens and comes to a boil.
3. Remove from heat and stir in vanilla extract and butter until smooth.
4. Pour the pudding into individual serving dishes and refrigerate for at least 2 hours.

Instructions for Whipped Cream:

1. In a chilled bowl, beat the heavy cream, powdered sugar, and vanilla extract until stiff peaks form.

2. Spoon the whipped cream on top of the chilled pudding before serving.